U.S.A. TRAVEL GUIDES

PENNSYLVANIA

BY ANN HEINRICHS • ILLUSTRATED BY MATT KANIA

Published by The Child's World®
1980 Lookout Drive • Mankato, MN 56003-1705
800-599-READ • www.childsworld.com

Photo Credits

Photographs ©: Shutterstock Images, cover, 1, 12, 37
(top), 37 (bottom); fishhawk CC2.0, 7; Gene J. Puskar/AP
Images, 8, 35; Charles Fox/Philadelphia Inquirer/MCT/
Newscom, 11; Paul Brady Photo/Shutterstock Images,
15; National Park Service, 16; Joseph-Siffrède Duplessis/
Library of Congress, 17; uniquelycat (Cathy) Smith CC2.0,
19; Life Atlas Photography/Shutterstock Images, 20;
Everett Historical/Shutterstock Images, 23; Library of
Congress, 24, 26; Nate Guidry/Pittsburgh Post-Gazette/
AP Images, 27; Nagel Photography/Shutterstock Images,
28; Ralph Francello/The Citizens' Voice/AP Images, 31;
Ambrose Little CC2.0, 32

ISBN 9781503819788
LCCN 2016961191

Printing

Printed in the United States of America
PA02334

Ann Heinrichs is the author
of more than 100 books
for children and young
adults. She has also enjoyed
successful careers as a
children's book editor and
an advertising copywriter.
Ann grew up in Fort Smith,
Arkansas, and lives in
Chicago, Illinois.

About the Author
Ann Heinrichs

Matt Kania loves maps and, as a
kid, dreamed of making them. In
school he studied geography and
cartography, and today he makes
maps for a living. Matt's favorite
thing about drawing maps is
learning about the places they
represent. Many of the maps
he has created can be found in
books, magazines, videos, Web
sites, and public places.

About the Map
Illustrator
Matt Kania

*On the cover: Independence Hall is a
must-see site in Pennsylvania.*

OUR PENNSYLVANIA TRIP

Pennsylvania. 4

Pine Creek Gorge near Wellsboro 7

Punxsutawney Phil. .8

The Roasting Ears of Corn Festival in Allentown 11

Lancaster's Amish Farm and House 12

Valley Forge and the Revolutionary War. 15

Historic Philadelphia. 16

Erie's U.S. Brig *Niagara* 19

Gettysburg and the Civil War 20

Tour-Ed Mine in Tarentum 23

Trains at Altoona's Horseshoe Curve 24

Pittsburgh's Carnegie Science Center 27

The State Capitol in Harrisburg 28

The Pittston Tomato Festival. 31

Hershey's Chocolate World 32

The Little League World Series 35

Our Trip 36

State Symbols. 37

State Song. 37

State Flag and Seal 37

Famous People. 38

Words to Know 38

To Learn More. 39

Index. 40

PENNSYLVANIA

Let's take a trip through Pennsylvania. You'll have some great adventures there!

You'll board a sailing ship and tour a mine. You'll see battlefields and soldiers' huts. You'll learn about Benjamin Franklin and Andrew Carnegie. You'll stand right next to the Liberty Bell. You'll explore mountains, forests, and **canyons**. You'll tour a chocolate factory. And you'll meet a friendly groundhog named Phil!

Are you ready? Then settle in and buckle up. Pennsylvania, here we come!

WELCOME TO PENNSYLVANIA

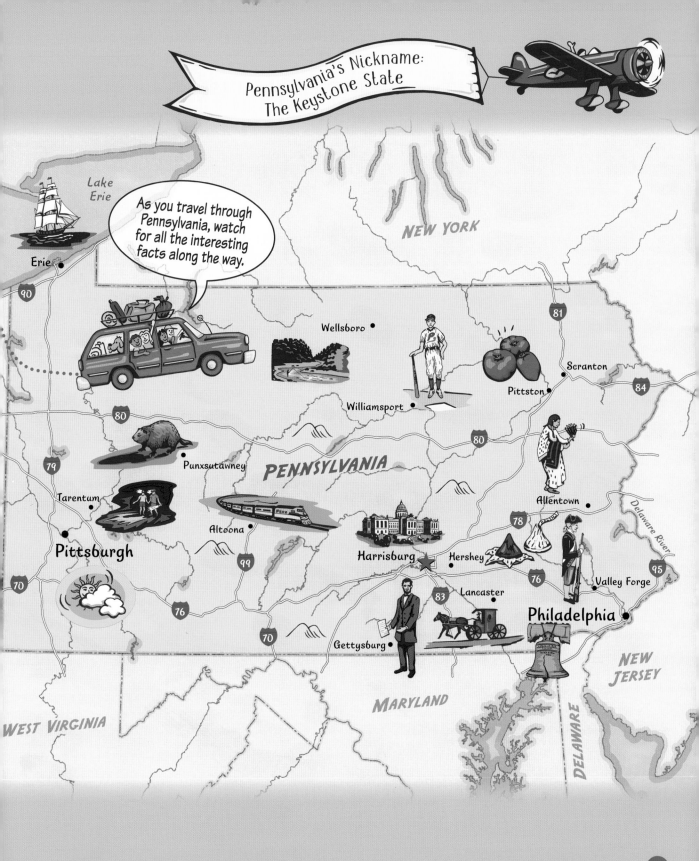

PINE CREEK GORGE NEAR WELLSBORO

Stand atop a rocky ridge. Then look down the mountainside. Rushing waters are roaring hundreds of feet below.

You're gazing down Pine Creek Gorge. It's on the Allegheny **Plateau**. This region covers northern and western Pennsylvania. The Allegheny Mountains rise at its eastern edge. The Allegheny Plateau and the Allegheny Mountains are part of the Appalachian Mountain range.

The Pocono Mountains are in northeastern Pennsylvania. They have many beautiful waterfalls. The land in the southeast is lower.

Three rivers come together in Pittsburgh. They're the Ohio, Allegheny, and Monongahela Rivers. The Delaware River forms Pennsylvania's eastern border.

Explore scenic hiking and biking trails at Pine Creek Gorge.

Furry little Phil pokes his head out. He looks around and squints. Then he goes back into his hole. Too bad. Six more weeks of winter!

This famous groundhog is Punxsutawney Phil. People watch him on Groundhog Day, which is February 2. Will he see his shadow? If he doesn't, spring is coming. What if he sees it? Then winter's staying for six more weeks!

Many other animals live in Pennsylvania. There are deer, rabbits, wild turkeys, and raccoons. Even black bears roam the woods. But only Phil predicts the weather!

Punxsutawney Phil lives on Gobbler's Knob in Punxsutawney.

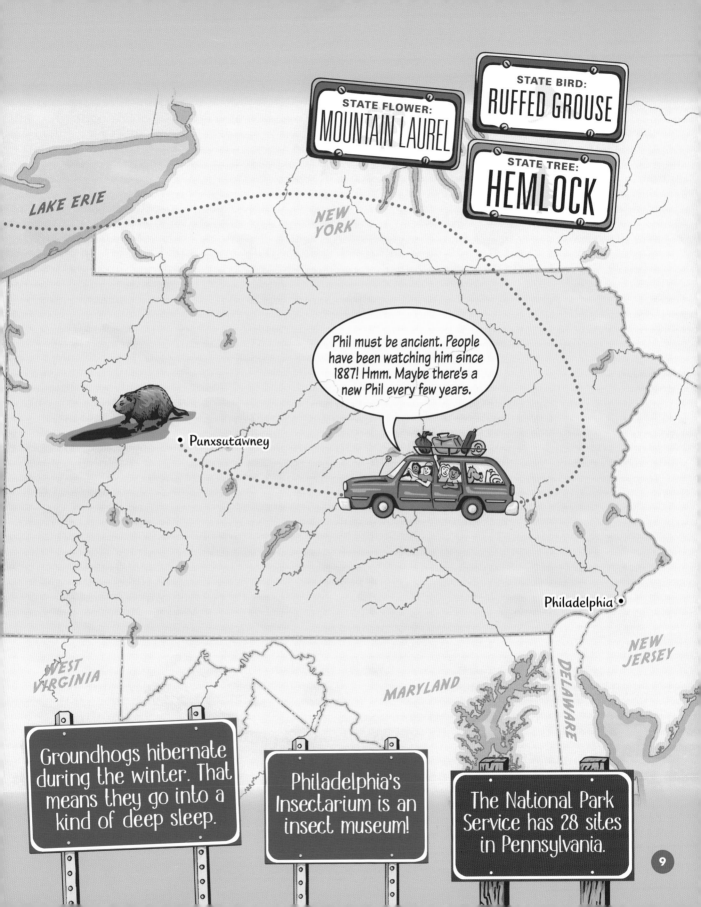

Who Lived Here before Europeans Arrived? Algonquian (Conoy, Lenni-Lenape, Nanticoke, Shawnee) and Iroquois (Susquehannock)

Pennsbury Manor in Morrisville was once William Penn's home.

LAKE ERIE

NEW YORK

Yum! I think I'll try a buffalo burger and some fire-roasted corn.

OHIO

Allentown •

Morrisville •

WEST VIRGINIA

MARYLAND

DELAWARE

NEW JERSEY

Colonists fought with French settlers and Native Americans. This was called the French and Indian War (1754-1763).

William Penn gave Pennsylvania its name. He used the name *Penn*, after his father, and *sylvania*, from *sylvan*. *Sylvan* means "woods" in Latin.

THE ROASTING EARS OF CORN FESTIVAL IN ALLENTOWN

The dancers wear feathers and colorful beads. Some of the feathers look like big wings. You're watching Native American performers at the Roasting Ears of Corn Festival. Some performers belong to the Nanticoke Lenni-Lenape Tribal Nation. The Lenni-Lenape and many other Native American groups gather at this festival every August. You'll find it at the Museum of Indian Culture in Allentown.

The Lenni-Lenape are also called the Delaware. They've lived in Pennsylvania for hundreds of years. Englishman William Penn arrived in 1682. He bought land from the Native Americans. He then founded the Pennsylvania **Colony**. It was one of 13 British colonies.

More than 50,000 Native Americans live in Pennsylvania today.

LANCASTER'S AMISH FARM AND HOUSE

Stroll around the farm. You'll see the windmill and barns. Cows and horses are grazing. The **blacksmith** is busy making horseshoes. Then visit the farmhouse. Wooden benches are set up for church services. Simple, dark clothes hang in the bedroom.

You're visiting the Amish Farm and House in Lancaster. The Amish are a Christian religious group. They're sometimes called the Pennsylvania Dutch. William Penn welcomed them to Pennsylvania.

The Amish dress and live in a simple way. They don't use electricity or modern machines. They make most of the things they need. They believe that living simply brings them closer to their faith. They are a close community. They help their neighbors with chores.

Many Amish people in Pennsylvania are farmers.

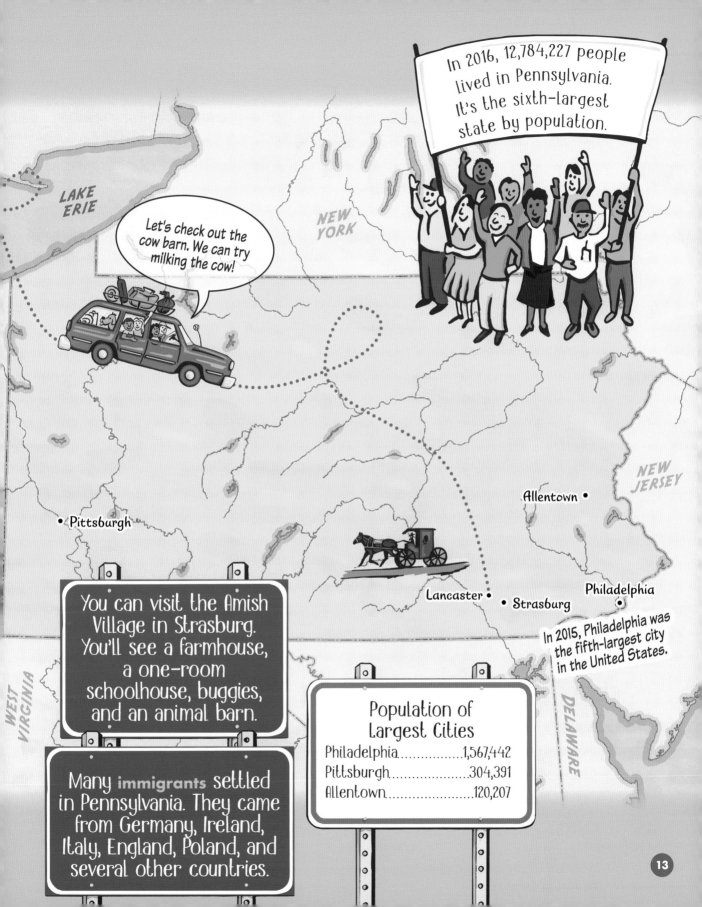

In 2016, 12,784,227 people lived in Pennsylvania. It's the sixth-largest state by population.

LAKE ERIE

NEW YORK

Let's check out the cow barn. We can try milking the cow!

NEW JERSEY

Allentown

• Pittsburgh

Lancaster • • Strasburg

Philadelphia

In 2015, Philadelphia was the fifth-largest city in the United States.

WEST VIRGINIA

DELAWARE

You can visit the Amish Village in Strasburg. You'll see a farmhouse, a one-room schoolhouse, buggies, and an animal barn.

Many immigrants settled in Pennsylvania. They came from Germany, Ireland, Italy, England, Poland, and several other countries.

Population of Largest Cities
Philadelphia..............1,567,442
Pittsburgh..................304,391
Allentown....................120,207

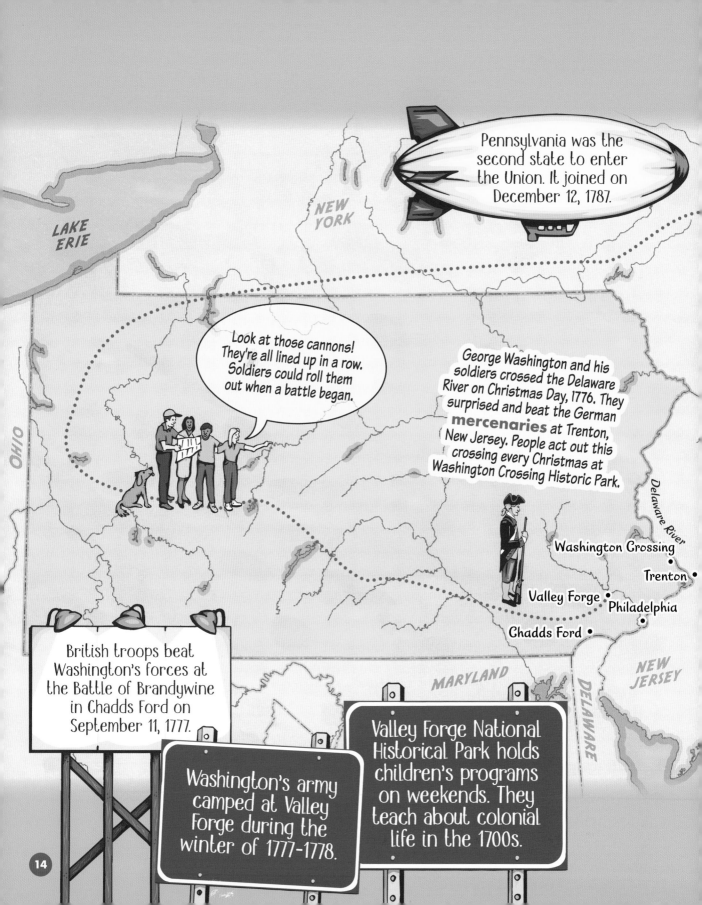

Pennsylvania was the second state to enter the Union. It joined on December 12, 1787.

Look at those cannons! They're all lined up in a row. Soldiers could roll them out when a battle began.

George Washington and his soldiers crossed the Delaware River on Christmas Day, 1776. They surprised and beat the German **mercenaries** at Trenton, New Jersey. People act out this crossing every Christmas at Washington Crossing Historic Park.

British troops beat Washington's forces at the Battle of Brandywine in Chadds Ford on September 11, 1777.

Washington's army camped at Valley Forge during the winter of 1777-1778.

Valley Forge National Historical Park holds children's programs on weekends. They teach about colonial life in the 1700s.

LAKE ERIE

NEW YORK

OHIO

Delaware River

Washington Crossing

Trenton

Valley Forge

Philadelphia

Chadds Ford

MARYLAND

DELAWARE

NEW JERSEY

VALLEY FORGE AND THE REVOLUTIONARY WAR

The colonists grew to hate British taxes. Colonial leaders formed the Continental Congress. They met in Philadelphia in 1774. Some colonists wanted to stay friendly with Britain. Others wanted to fight Britain for freedom. Soon the Revolutionary War (1775–1783) broke out.

General George Washington led the colonial army. Washington's army camped at Valley Forge one winter. It was bitterly cold, and supplies were low. Many soldiers died there.

You can visit Valley Forge today. You'll see the soldiers' log huts. You'll discover what daily life was like for people living in the camp.

The colonial army beat the British at last. The colonies became the United States of America.

Reenactors dressed as Revolutionary War soldiers march into Valley Forge.

Stand beside the Liberty Bell. It's bigger than you! And it weighs more than dozens of kids.

This big bell is in Independence National Historical Park. That's Philadelphia's old section. You'll see many historic buildings there. One is Independence Hall. The Declaration of Independence was signed there. The U.S. Constitution was written there, too. The Constitution states the country's basic ideas and laws.

The First Continental Congress met in nearby Carpenters' Hall. Just walk along the streets. You'll learn about history without even trying!

The Liberty Bell weighs more than 2,000 pounds (907 kg)!

Dear Mr. Franklin:

You published the *Pennsylvania Gazette* newspaper. You wrote articles calling for independence. You also signed the Declaration of Independence. Thanks for helping the country become free!

Sincerely,

Poor Richard

Mr. Benjamin Franklin
1706-1790
Philadelphia, PA

Look at that big crack in the Liberty Bell! It cracked in 1846 when people rang it during a celebration of George Washington's birthday.

Benjamin Franklin and some friends founded the first subscription library in the colonies in 1731.

Benjamin Franklin's writings helped stir up feelings for freedom. Franklin also wrote *Poor Richard's Almanack.* It was full of wise sayings. A section of Independence Park teaches about Franklin's life and work.

Betsy Ross's house is in Philadelphia. Ross sewed together the first U.S. flag.

Thomas Jefferson wrote most of the Declaration of Independence. You can visit Philadelphia's Declaration House, where he wrote it.

Philadelphia was the country's capital city from 1790 to 1800.

NEW YORK

E ERIE

Philadelphia

MARYLAND

DELAWARE

NEW JERSEY

LAKE ERIE

NEW YORK

Presque Isle

Erie

OHIO

WEST VIRGINIA

MARYLAND

NEW JERSEY

The Erie Maritime Museum is near *Niagara's* port. There you'll learn all about the Battle of Lake Erie.

Let's check out the ship. Then let's go to Erie's ExpERIEnce Children's Museum! We'll learn more about Lake Erie and other Great Lakes.

Presque Isle is a sandy **peninsula** near Erie. It reaches out into Lake Erie. Presque Isle is French for "almost an island."

The Battle of Lake Erie took place on September 10, 1813.

A brig is a sailing ship with two masts and square sails.

ERIE'S U.S. BRIG *NIAGARA*

Climb aboard the *Niagara*. It's a sailing ship called a brig. Then imagine you're fighting a sea battle. This ship won a famous battle in 1813.

Commodore Oliver Hazard Perry commanded the *Niagara*. He was fighting in the War of 1812 (1812–1815). Perry beat several British ships on Lake Erie. Then he made his famous report: "We have met the enemy, and they are ours."

The town of Erie is best known for building the ships used in this battle. But there's a lot to do in Erie. Many people enjoy its sandy lakeshore. They play in the sand and waves.

There goes the Niagara! *Wave to the crew as it sets sail!*

L ook out over the rolling fields of Gettysburg. Thousands of soldiers died here. They were fighting the Civil War (1861–1865). Northern and Southern states fought this war over slavery.

Pennsylvania and other Northern states opposed slavery. Southern states wanted to keep slavery. This led to war. The North formed the Union side. Southern states pulled away and formed the Confederacy.

A bloody, three-day battle took place at Gettysburg. Part of the battlefield was made into a cemetery. President Abraham Lincoln spoke there. His famous speech is called the Gettysburg Address.

You can take a guided bus tour of Gettysburg Battlefield or explore the site on foot.

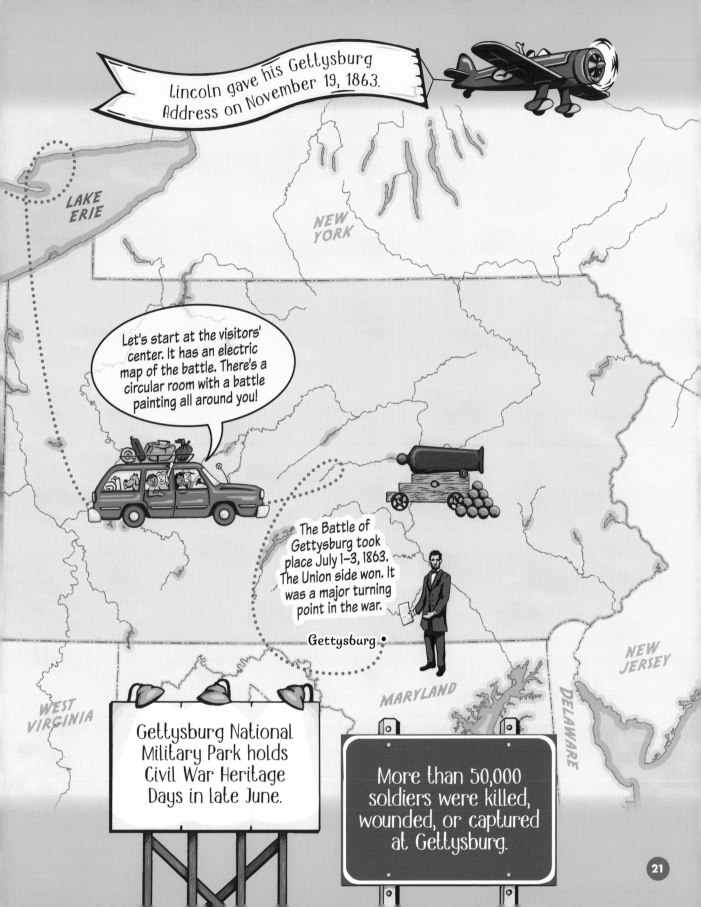

Lincoln gave his Gettysburg Address on November 19, 1863.

Let's start at the visitors' center. It has an electric map of the battle. There's a circular room with a battle painting all around you!

The Battle of Gettysburg took place July 1–3, 1863. The Union side won. It was a major turning point in the war.

LAKE ERIE

NEW YORK

Gettysburg

MARYLAND

WEST VIRGINIA

NEW JERSEY

DELAWARE

Gettysburg National Military Park holds Civil War Heritage Days in late June.

More than 50,000 soldiers were killed, wounded, or captured at Gettysburg.

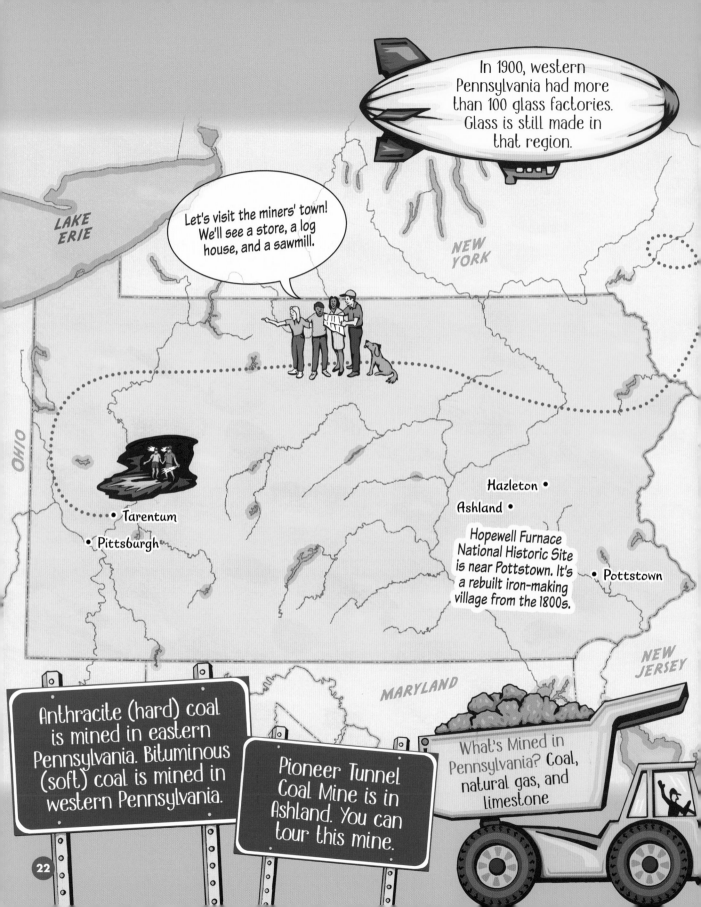

In 1900, western Pennsylvania had more than 100 glass factories. Glass is still made in that region.

Let's visit the miners' town! We'll see a store, a log house, and a sawmill.

LAKE ERIE

NEW YORK

OHIO

Hazleton •

Ashland •

Hopewell Furnace National Historic Site is near Pottstown. It's a rebuilt iron-making village from the 1800s.

• Pottstown

• Tarentum

• Pittsburgh

NEW JERSEY

MARYLAND

Anthracite (hard) coal is mined in eastern Pennsylvania. Bituminous (soft) coal is mined in western Pennsylvania.

Pioneer Tunnel Coal Mine is in Ashland. You can tour this mine.

What's Mined in Pennsylvania? Coal, natural gas, and limestone

TOUR-ED MINE IN TARENTUM

First put on your hard hat. Then go deep into the coal mine. A real miner shows you how miners once worked. You're visiting the Tour-Ed Mine in Tarentum!

Pennsylvania's coal **industry** grew after the Civil War. Miners dug tons of coal from the ground. Railroads carried the coal to major cities.

Factories began using coal as a fuel. This helped the iron and steel industries grow. Pittsburgh soon became the country's top steelmaker. Other factories made leather, cloth, glass, and cement.

The state is still a top coal producer. Pennsylvania also mines iron, oil, and natural gas.

Miners prepare for a day of work at a coal mine in Hazleton in the early 1900s.

TRAINS AT ALTOONA'S HORSESHOE CURVE

Toot, toot! Clank, clank! Around the curve they come. The trains are screeching around Horseshoe Curve near Altoona. Just hop on the hillside train car. Then ride up the hill. You'll have a great view of the curving tracks.

It was hard to build train tracks here. The Allegheny Mountains are really steep. Workers built the tracks in big loopy curves. That way, trains could climb the steep slopes.

Horseshoe Curve opened for train travel in 1854. At last, trains could get over the mountains. Then people could ship goods across the state.

All aboard! A train travels along Horseshoe Curve in the early 1900s.

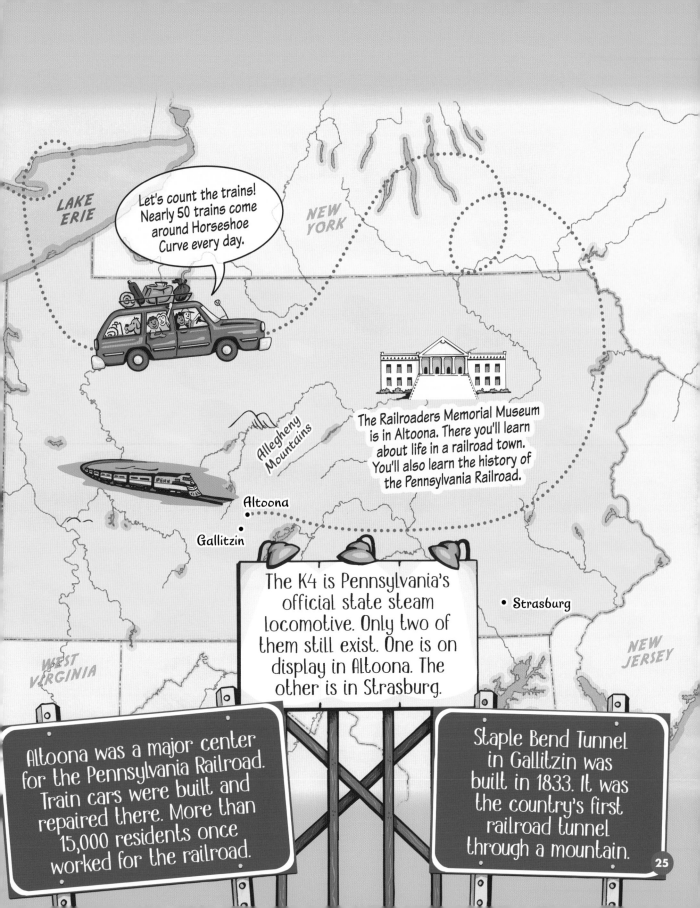

Let's count the trains! Nearly 50 trains come around Horseshoe Curve every day.

The Railroaders Memorial Museum is in Altoona. There you'll learn about life in a railroad town. You'll also learn the history of the Pennsylvania Railroad.

The K4 is Pennsylvania's official state steam locomotive. Only two of them still exist. One is on display in Altoona. The other is in Strasburg.

Altoona was a major center for the Pennsylvania Railroad. Train cars were built and repaired there. More than 15,000 residents once worked for the railroad.

Staple Bend Tunnel in Gallitzin was built in 1833. It was the country's first railroad tunnel through a mountain.

LAKE ERIE

NEW YORK

Allegheny Mountains

Altoona

Gallitzin

Strasburg

WEST VIRGINIA

NEW JERSEY

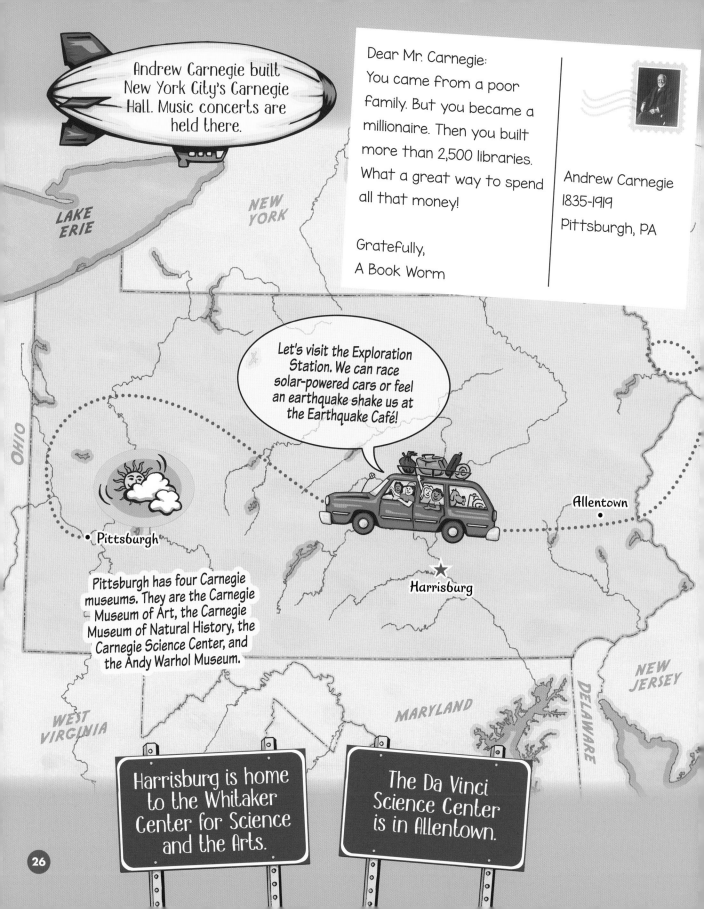

Andrew Carnegie built New York City's Carnegie Hall. Music concerts are held there.

Dear Mr. Carnegie:
You came from a poor family. But you became a millionaire. Then you built more than 2,500 libraries. What a great way to spend all that money!

Gratefully,
A Book Worm

Andrew Carnegie
1835-1919
Pittsburgh, PA

LAKE ERIE

NEW YORK

OHIO

Let's visit the Exploration Station. We can race solar-powered cars or feel an earthquake shake us at the Earthquake Café!

Allentown

Pittsburgh

Pittsburgh has four Carnegie museums. They are the Carnegie Museum of Art, the Carnegie Museum of Natural History, the Carnegie Science Center, and the Andy Warhol Museum.

Harrisburg

WEST VIRGINIA

MARYLAND

DELAWARE

NEW JERSEY

Harrisburg is home to the Whitaker Center for Science and the Arts.

The Da Vinci Science Center is in Allentown.

Design and launch a rocket. Learn about robotics. See hissing cockroaches and learn how weather works. You're exploring the Carnegie Science Center in Pittsburgh!

This museum is named after Andrew Carnegie. He formed his Carnegie Steel Company in 1899. Many of its mills were in the Pittsburgh area. Pittsburgh became a major steelmaking center. Many famous buildings were made with Pittsburgh steel. Carnegie sold his steel company in 1901. It grew into today's U.S. Steel Corporation.

Carnegie made millions of dollars. He gave much of that money to charity. It was used for building museums and libraries.

Visitors learn about liquids and solids at the Carnegie Science Center.

THE STATE CAPITOL IN HARRISBURG

You'll love visiting the state capitol in Harrisburg. It looks like a grand palace! Just walk into the big, round central area. Look up, and you'll see almost 4,000 lights. Above you rises the huge, curved dome.

This is the main state government building. Pennsylvania has three branches of government. One branch makes the laws. Its members meet in the capitol. Another branch carries out the laws. It's headed by the governor. Judges make up the third branch. They study the laws. Then they decide whether someone has broken a law.

How would you like to work here? Pennsylvania lawmakers meet in the capitol.

Wow! Look at that dome. It weighs 52 million pounds (24 million kg)! It won't fall, will it?

Some areas of the capitol have tile floors. The tiles show scenes of wildlife, industry, farming, and historical events.

Pennsylvania's official name is the **Commonwealth** of Pennsylvania. Kentucky, Massachusetts, and Virginia are also called commonwealths.

Welcome to Harrisburg, the capital of Pennsylvania!

James Buchanan (1791-1868) was the 15th president. He was born near Mercersburg.

Pennsylvania's state motto is "Virtue, Liberty, and Independence."

THE PITTSTON TOMATO FESTIVAL

Watch out! Here comes a big one! Splat! Yuck!

You tried to duck out of the way. But you didn't duck fast enough. You've joined the big tomato fight! It's an event at the Pittston Tomato Festival.

Pittston is proud of its tomatoes. Lots of farmers in the area grow them. Mushrooms are the state's top crop, though. Pennsylvania grows more mushrooms than any other state. Corn and hay are important, too. Most of the corn becomes cattle feed.

Dairy cattle graze across eastern Pennsylvania. They produce tons of milk. Chickens and eggs are valuable farm products, too.

The Pittston Tomato Festival's tomato fight can get messy!

HERSHEY'S CHOCOLATE WORLD

Do you like chocolate? Then you'll love Hershey's Chocolate World. Guess what city it's in. Hershey! You can take a chocolate-making tour there.

First you'll walk through a jungle. Cocoa beans are growing there. Then you'll see how cocoa beans are made into chocolate. Finally, you'll get to eat some delicious samples. Yum!

Foods are important factory goods in Pennsylvania. Food plants make chocolate, bread, cookies, and pretzels. Some factories package mushrooms and meats. Chemicals are the state's leading factory products. They include medicine and paint. Crayola crayons are made in Pennsylvania, too!

Hershey Foods has one of the world's largest chocolate and cocoa factories.

You can tour the Harley-Davidson motorcycle factory in York.

LAKE ERIE

NEW YORK

What's Made in Pennsylvania? Chemicals, food products, electronic equipment, and fabricated metal products

Give me some Kisses! No, Mom, not that kind. I want Hershey's Kisses!

Easton

Allentown

The U.S. Mint in Philadelphia makes coins and medals.

Hershey

The Hershey Museum in Hershey has exhibits on the town, the candy, and Milton Hershey, who founded the chocolate company.

York

Philadelphia

WEST VIRGINIA

MARYLAND

NEW JERSEY

DELAWARE

Visit the Crayola crayon factory in Easton. It makes almost three billion crayons each year!

Do you like big Mack Trucks? You can learn more about them at the Mack Trucks Historical Museum in Allentown.

Do you like amusement parks with thrilling rides? Pennsylvania has 14 parks like this!

What if you played baseball on Mars? Your balls would travel farther, and you could jump three times as high!

LAKE ERIE

NEW YORK

OHIO

Williamsport • • South Williamsport

The World of Little League: Peter J. McGovern Museum and Official Stores is in South Williamsport. It features displays and hands-on exhibits on the history of Little League baseball.

Pittsburgh

Pennsylvania has more than 1,000 museums and hundreds of historical sites.

Philadelphia

NEW JERSEY

WEST VIRGINIA

PENNSYLVANIA SPORTS TEAMS
Philadelphia 76ers (basketball)
Philadelphia Eagles (football)
Philadelphia Flyers (hockey)
Philadelphia Phillies (baseball)

PENNSYLVANIA SPORTS TEAMS
Pittsburgh Penguins (hockey)
Pittsburgh Pirates (baseball)
Pittsburgh Steelers (football)

THE LITTLE LEAGUE WORLD SERIES

Kids are here from Mexico, Europe, and Asia. They're all ready to play baseball. It's the Little League World Series!

Little League baseball began in Williamsport in 1939. In time, it spread all over the world. Now Williamsport holds the Little League World Series. Some of the world's best players take part.

Pennsylvanians enjoy big-league sports, too. But many people have fun in other ways. They go swimming or hiking. They climb mountains or trek through forests. Some like visiting historic sites and museums. There's something for everyone in Pennsylvania!

A New York team plays against a South Korean team in the 2016 Little League World Series.

OUR TRIP

We visited many amazing places on our trip! We also met a lot of interesting people along the way. Look at the map below. Use your finger to trace all the places we have been.

What is called the Grand Canyon of Pennsylvania? *See page 6 for the answer.*

How long have people been watching Punxsutawney Phil? *Page 9 has the answer.*

When did Pennsylvania enter the Union? *See page 14 for the answer.*

When did the Liberty Bell crack? *Look on page 17 for the answer.*

How many Carnegie museums are in Pittsburgh? *Page 26 has the answer.*

What is Pennsylvania's state motto? *Turn to page 29 for the answer.*

What Pennsylvania town holds a mushroom festival? *Look on page 30 for the answer.*

How many Crayola crayons are produced each year? *Turn to page 33 for the answer.*

STATE SYMBOLS

State animal: White-tailed deer

State beautification plant: Crown vetch

State beverage: Milk

State bird: Ruffed grouse

State dog: Great Dane

State electric locomotive: GGI 4859 electric locomotive

State fish: Brook trout

State flower: Mountain laurel

State fossil: *Phacops rana*

State insect: Firefly

State ship: U.S. brig *Niagara*

State steam locomotive: K4 steam locomotive

State tree: Hemlock

STATE SONG

"PENNSYLVANIA"

Words and music by Eddie Khoury and Ronnie Bonner

Pennsylvania, Pennsylvania,
Mighty is your name,
Steeped in glory and tradition,
Object of acclaim.
Where brave men fought the
    foe of freedom,
Tyranny decried,
'Til the bell of independence
Filled the countryside.

Chorus:
Pennsylvania, Pennsylvania,
May your future be

filled with honor everlasting
as your history.

Pennsylvania, Pennsylvania,
Blessed by God's own hand,
Birthplace of a mighty nation,
Keystone of the land.
Where first our country's flag
    unfolded,
Freedom to proclaim,
May the voices of tomorrow
glorify your name.

(Chorus)

State seal

That was a great trip! We have traveled all over Pennsylvania. There are a few places we didn't have time for, though. Next time, we plan to visit the Houdini Museum in Scranton. Visitors learn all about famous magician and escape artist Harry Houdini. The museum features items related to Houdini's life and career. Some date back to the late 1800s!

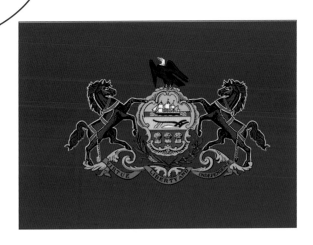

State flag

FAMOUS PEOPLE

Anderson, Marian (1897–1993), concert singer

Biden, Joe (1942–), former U.S. vice president

Brown, Marc (1946–), children's author and illustrator

Buchanan, James (1791–1868), 15th U.S. president

Carson, Rachel (1907–1964), author and environmentalist

Cassatt, Mary (1844–1926), painter

Catalanotto, Peter (1959–), children's author and illustrator

Fey, Tina (1970–), actress and comedian

Franklin, Benjamin (1706–1790), inventor, author, and patriot during the American Revolution

Hershey, Milton S. (1857–1945), founder of the Hershey Chocolate Company

Jackson, Reggie (1946–), baseball player

Kelly, Gene (1912–1996), dancer and actor

Mead, Margaret (1901–1978), anthropologist

Montana, Joe (1956–), football player

Mott, Lucretia (1793–1880), leader of the abolitionist and women's rights movements

Palmer, Arnold (1929–2016), golfer

Penn, William (1644–1718), founder of Pennsylvania

Rogers, Fred (1928–2003), children's TV show host "Mr. Rogers"

Ross, Betsy (1752–1836), patriot during the American Revolution

Smith, Will (1968–), actor and rapper

Stewart, James (1908–1997), actor

Swift, Taylor (1989–), singer and musician

WORDS TO KNOW

blacksmith (BLAK-smith) someone who makes metal objects using fire to heat the metal and a hammer to shape it

canyons (KAN-yuhnz) deep valleys worn through by rivers

colonists (KOL-uh-nists) people who settle a new land for their home country

colony (KOL-uh-nee) a land with ties to a parent country

commonwealth (KOM-uhn-welth) a state or nation founded for the people's common good

immigrants (IM-uh-gruhnts) people who leave their home country and move to another country

industry (IN-duh-stree) a type of business

mercenaries (MUR-suh-ner-eez) soldiers who are paid to fight for a foreign army

peninsula (puh-NIN-suh-luh) a piece of land that is almost entirely surrounded by water

plateau (pla-TOH) land that is high and somewhat level

TO LEARN MORE

IN THE LIBRARY

DeMocker, Michael. *The Lenape.* Kennett Square, PA: Purple Toad, 2016.

Friesen, Helen Lepp. *Pennsylvania: The Keystone State.* New York, NY: AV2 by Weigl, 2013.

Martin, David. *The Colony of Pennsylvania.* New York, NY: PowerKids, 2015.

ON THE WEB

Visit our Web site for links about Pennsylvania:

childsworld.com/links

Note to Parents, Teachers, and Librarians: We routinely verify our Web links to make sure they are safe and active sites. So encourage your readers to check them out!

PLACES TO VISIT OR CONTACT
Pennsylvania Historical and Museum Commission

phmc.pa.gov
300 North Street
Harrisburg, PA 17120
717/787-3362
For more information about the history of Pennsylvania

Visit Pennsylvania

visitpa.com
400 North Street, Fourth Floor
Harrisburg, PA 17120
800/847-4872
For more information about traveling in Pennsylvania

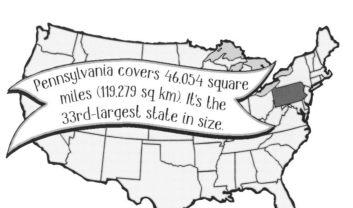

Pennsylvania covers 46,054 square miles (119,279 sq km). It's the 33rd-largest state in size.

INDEX

A

Allegheny Mountains, 7, 24
Allegheny Plateau, 7
Allegheny River, 7
Allentown, 11, 13, 26, 33
Altoona, 24–25
Amish culture, 12–13
Amish Farm and House, 12
amusement parks, 34
Appalachian Mountains, 7
Ashland, 22

B

Battle of Brandywine, 14
Battle of Lake Erie, 18
Buchanan, James, 29

C

Carnegie, Andrew, 26–27
Carnegie Science Center, 26–27
Carnegie Steel Company, 27
Carpenters' Hall, 16
Chadds Ford, 14
chemical industry, 32
Civil War, 20–21, 23
Civil War Heritage Days, 21
climate, 6
coal industry, 22–23
colonists, 10, 15
Continental Congress, 15, 16
Crayola crayon factory, 33

D

dairy farming, 30–31
Da Vinci Science Center, 26
Declaration House, 17
Declaration of Independence, 16–17
Delaware people. *See* Lenni-Lenape people.
Delaware River, 6–7, 14
Delaware Water Gap, 6

E

elevation, 6
English exploration, 11
Erie, 18–19

F

farming, 12, 29, 30–31
Franklin, Benjamin, 17
French and Indian War, 10

G

Gallitzin, 25
Gettysburg, 20–21
Gettysburg Address, 20
Gettysburg National Military Park, 21
glass industry, 22–23
Gobbler's Knob, 9
Grand Canyon, 6
Great Lakes, 6, 18
groundhog, 8–9
Groundhog Day, 8

H

Harley-Davidson motorcycle factory, 33
Harrisburg, 26, 28–29
Hershey, 32–33
Hershey, Milton, 33
Hershey Museum, 33
Hershey's Chocolate World, 32
Horseshoe Curve, 24–25

I

immigrants, 13
Independence Hall, 16
Independence National Historical Park, 16
industries, 22–23, 27, 32–33
Insectarium, 9
iron industry, 22–23

J

Jefferson, Thomas, 17

K

Kennett Square, 30

L

Lake Erie, 6, 18–19
Lancaster, 12
Lenni-Lenape people, 10–11
Liberty Bell, 16–17

Lincoln, Abraham, 20–21
Little League World Series, 35

M

Mack Trucks, 33
Mercersburg, 29
mines, 22–23
Monongahela River, 7
Mount Davis, 6
Museum of Indian Culture, 11
museums, 9, 11, 18, 25, 26–27, 33, 34–35
mushrooms, 30–31, 32

N

national parks, 9, 14, 16, 21
Native Americans, 10–11
Niagara (brig ship), 18–19

O

Ohio River, 7

P

Penn, William, 10–11, 12
Pennsylvania Colony, 11
Pennsylvania Dutch. *See* Amish culture.
Pennsylvania Railroad, 25
Perry, Oliver Hazard, 19
Perrydell Farm Dairy, 30
Philadelphia, 9, 13, 15, 16–17, 33
Pine Creek Gorge, 6–7
Pioneer Tunnel Coal Mine, 22
Pittsburgh, 7, 13, 23, 26–27
Pittston, 30–31
Pittston Tomato Festival, 30–31
Pocono Mountains, 7
Poor Richard's Almanack, 17
population, 13
Presque Isle, 18
Punxsutawney, 8–9
Punxsutawney Phil, 8–9

R

railroads, 23, 25
Revolutionary War, 14–15
Roasting Ears of Corn Festival, 11
Ross, Betsy, 17

S

settlers, 10
slavery, 20
South Williamsport, 34
sports, 34–35
Staple Bend Tunnel, 25
state bird, 9
state capital, 29
state capitol, 28–29
state flower, 9
state government, 28
state motto, 29
state name, 10, 29
state nickname, 5
state steam locomotive, 25
state tree, 9
steel industry, 23, 27
Strasburg, 13, 25

T

Tarentum, 23
Tour-Ed Mine, 23

U

United States Constitution, 16
U.S. Steel Corporation, 27

V

Valley Forge, 14–15
Valley Forge National Historical Park, 14

W

War of 1812, 19
Washington, George, 14–15, 17
Wellsboro, 7
Whitaker Center for Science and the Arts, 26
Williamsport, 35

Y

York, 30, 33

Bye, Keystone State. We had a great time. We'll come back soon!